THE JESSL

THE JESSE TREE

Daily Readings for Advent

Thom M Shuman

WILD GOOSE PUBLICATIONS

www.ionabooks.com

Published by
Wild Goose Publications
4th Floor, Savoy House, 140 Sauchiehall St, Glasgow G2 3DH, UK
web: www.ionabooks.com
Wild Goose Publications is the publishing division of the Iona Community. Scottish
Charity No. SCO03794. Limited Company Reg. No. SCO96243.

ISBN 1 905010 06 0

A catalogue record for this book is available from the British Library.

Overseas distribution
Australia: Willow Connection Pty Ltd, Unit 4A, 3-9 Kenneth Road,
Manly Vale, NSW 2093
New Zealand: Pleroma, Higginson Street, Otane 4170,
Central Hawkes Bay
Canada: Bayard Distribution, 49 Front Street East, Toronto, Ontario M5E 1B3

Permission to reproduce any part of this work in Australia or New Zealand should
be sought from Willow Connection.

Printed by Bell & Bain, Thornliebank, Glasgow, UK

CONTENTS

INTRODUCTION

The first time I encountered a Jesse tree was as a kid in Sunday school, with the teacher using a flannel board on which different symbols were placed to represent the people in the 'family tree' of Jesus. There was a harp for David, an apple for Adam and Eve, a piece of multi-coloured fabric for the coat Joseph wore, and so on. The scriptural basis for this idea comes from Isaiah 11:1. 'A shoot shall come out from the stump of Jesse, and a branch shall grow out of his roots.' Since Jesse was David's father, and Jesus was of the lineage of David, the Jesse tree became a way of teaching many of the Bible stories to children during the Advent season.

The nice thing about a Jesse tree is that a family can choose to use one for devotions during Advent, even if their church is not focusing on the Jesse tree. Over the years, I have seen Jesse trees take different forms. Some churches give each family a tree branch, usually two to three feet high, with lots of little branches attached. The branch can be placed in a bucket of rocks/earth, and then draped over with green cloth or paper. Another option is to cut the shape of a tree out of green or brown felt and to glue it to a piece of heavy cardboard. You can then glue little wooden pegs onto the 'tree' to hold the ornaments, or put Velcro on the back of the ornaments to make them stick. Some creative folks have taken the branch of a tree and suspended it from the ceiling (usually with fishing line), thus creating a Jesse tree mobile.

As the children in the church I am blessed to serve made Jesse trees last year, I could see their excitement and the joy they experienced in making the trees, the ornaments, and in hearing stories of some of the folks in the Bible who are ancestors of Jesus. And I thought: We know the familiar stories like Noah and the Ark; we know the famous people, like Mary and David – but what about those folks that Jesus might have heard about at bedtime? What about the people who might only be mentioned once in the Bible (in the lineages in Matthew and Luke)? What about the women, the prophets, the exiles who, while not linked to Jesus genetically, nevertheless passed on their 'spiritual DNA' to him and to us?

They are just as much a part of his heritage, his family, his 'tree' as all his relatives by blood and by marriage. They are a part of the tradition and faith we seek to pass on to our children and grandchildren.

They are branches on the Jesse tree.

Thom Shuman

FIRST

WEEK

WE'RE THINKING OF MOVING

Read Genesis 12:1–4a

As usual, Abe was late. The rest of the ROMEOs (Retired Old Men Eating Out) were on their second cup of coffee by the time he slipped into the lone empty chair. Gratefully accepting his steaming mug from Nancy, he slowly sipped as he listened to the weekly highlights of various kids and grandkids, and murmured appreciatively over the inevitable photos. As usual, he had no such stories to tell or pictures to share.

After breakfast orders had been placed, one of the men said, 'Abe, you're quieter than normal. Everything okay? Your nephew taking good care of the business?'

'Oh, Lot's doing a super job,' Abe replied. 'Based on the monthly cheque I get, I have no complaints there.'

'Sarie doing well?' another enquired.

'Other than her normal carping about wanting to move to a ranch-style house to stop climbing all those stairs, she's great,' Abe answered.

The silence that followed could have deafened a heavy metal band.

'C'mon, Abe! We've known you too long not to know there's something on your mind. Spill.'

'Well,' Abe let out a long sigh, 'we're thinking of moving.'

'Ah, finally getting rid of the old place, huh? Will you be moving to one of those fancy retirement villages?'

'No, not quite.'

'I'll bet he's gone and bought one of those caravans, and he and Sarie will be living and travelling in that.'

First Sunday of Advent

'No, that's not it either.'

'For heaven's sake, Abe, what then?'

'We're selling the house, Lot's selling the business, and we're all moving to Canaan.'

The silence that followed this time was enough to fill a cathedral.

'Canaan? Canaan ... I've heard of Canaan ... that's where ... that's ... Where is Canaan?' one of the newer members asked.

'I'll tell you,' exploded Abe's best friend. 'It's nowhere. You can't get there from here, even if you wanted to, which no one in his right mind would. It's the flea on the tail of the king's dog; it's the bottom of the worst cesspool you've ever smelled; it's the most godforsaken place in the world, and even the gods have lost the directions on how to find it. That's Canaan, brother, that's Canaan.'

'Then why, Abe, why there of all places?'

'Well,' he said with a slight smile on his lips, 'you might say someone told me to go there.'

Prayer

Where are you calling us to go, God? What risks are you asking us to take this Advent season? What steps might we take, even hesitantly, in order to follow you? Speak to us, God, speak to us. Amen

THE SKELETON IN THE CLOSET

Read Joshua 2:1–21; 6:17,23–25

Some people are born on the 'wrong' side of the tracks; Rahab lived on the right side of the gap – the space that separated the two walls which surrounded Jericho. Actually, her house was built so that it straddled the gap, though, in her case, it seems that her windows looked out from the outer wall. Scripture speaks of her as being a harlot or a prostitute, though she might have been an innkeeper (it's hard to tell since, back in her day, innkeepers were also called harlots, both trades being seen as morally deficient). Whatever the case, because of what she did for Joshua's spies, she became a 'player' in the movement of the people of Israel into the Promised Land, and a role model for faith. The writer of Hebrews names her and only one other woman (can you name her without looking?) in the great chapter on faith (Hebrews 11).

Rabbinic tradition tells us that Rahab, this outsider, was one of the four most beautiful women in the world, and was the ancestor of eight prophets (including Jeremiah) and one prophetess (Huldah). Not bad for someone the rest of society looked down their noses at! And if tradition is right that she married Salmon, one of the spies, then she became the mother of Boaz, and thus great-great grandmother of David, from whom Jesus is descended. Maybe this 'skeleton in the closet' is one of the reasons Jesus was so welcoming to prostitutes and other outsiders.

First Monday of Advent

Prayer

We all have 'skeletons' in our closet, Understanding God – folk we are just a little embarrassed about being a part of our family. Do we use them as an excuse to turn our backs on people like them, or an opportunity to be as forgiving and welcoming as Rahab's family member, Jesus? Help us to ponder such questions in this season, we pray. Amen

WHAT'S IN A NAME?

Read Matthew 1:14 (if you really want to, you could read all of Matthew 1:1–17!)

It didn't make the Top Ten, or the Hit Hundred, or even the most popular 1,000 names of 2003. In fact, it didn't even make the top 1,000 of the most popular names given to newborn boys in the last millennium!

Achim.

Not surprised, are you? After all, how many Achims have you known in your lifetime? You could count them all on one hair of your head (if even that many), I would bet. Yet there he is in the Bible, in the genealogy of Jesus – one of the ancestors of our Lord.

Was he a merchant, a shepherd, a carpenter? Did he have a big family? Did he love his children? Did he care for his wife? Was he a man of strong faith, or did he just attend synagogue occasionally? We don't know if there were any stories told to young Jesus about this person in his family tree.

He's like some of our ancestors in those family photographs taken so long ago; those tintypes stored too long in shoe boxes; those Kodak moments that fade over the years until they are all curled at the edges, the faces kind of blurry. 'Who is that, Mum, that guy standing in front of that funny car?' 'Who is that, Grandpa, who's holding you on her lap?'

And we look, and we think, and we wonder, and we stammer, 'I don't remember his name, but he was some sort of relation to my grandmother. She looks a lot like your Aunt Moira, but I'll be darned if I know who it is.'

But someone knew who these people were, and what they did, and what they meant to their families, to their children, to their friends, to their neighbours.

First Tuesday of Advent

We may not remember their names, but someone does, someone who knew Achim when he was a little boy, and a teenager, and an adult. Someone who watched over Achim from his birth to his death. Someone who continues to know him, and call him by name.

And it's the same One who knows us by name, and always will … the One we call God.

Prayer

As we write names on gift tags, we lift them up to you, Name above all names. As we address Christmas cards, we ask that you surround these people with your peace and joy. As we stick labels on packages, we pray that your love and hope will accompany ours on a journey of love to these people. You know us by name, O God, and never forget us, even when we forget you. Amen

THE LOSS OF INNOCENTS

Read Matthew 2:16–18 and Jeremiah 31:15

Yad Vashem (Memorial to the name)

Jacob
was going to shepherd
the children
and teach them
to love their neighbour
as passionately
as they loved the Lord;

Benjamin
would have been
a strong rabbi,
pointing his people
to the One
whose birthday he shared;

Josiah,
along with his older brother, Nicodemus,
might have swayed the Sanhedrin
towards a different judgement
that fateful night in Jerusalem;

but the streets of Bethlehem
are eerily silent today,

First Wednesday of Advent

and Ramah is washed
with the tears of Rachel
and all the other mothers.

Who weeps for the innocents
of Ramallah and Rhondda Cynon Taff;

who consoles the mothers
of Randwick and Fallujah;

who notices the silent streets
in Kabul and Kansas City?

Prayer

Innocent of Bethlehem, may we join you in wiping the tears, in walking the
empty streets, in bringing peace and reconciliation to the places of violence and
destruction. May this be our Advent prayer, and our Advent calling. Amen

AGAINST ALL THE ODDS

Read 2 Samuel 21:1–13

We've seen it played out over and over all too often – India, Northern Ireland, Palestine/Israel, the Ukraine ... Some person, some group, some religion, some nation does an injury to another, and sets in motion years, if not centuries, of life based on retribution and revenge.

There is a famine in the land in the early years of David's reign and it seems to be have been caused by something Saul did to the Gibeonites (who weren't liked to begin with because they had tricked Joshua into accepting them). And, acting before praying, David asks the Gibeonites (not God!) what he can do to atone for this foul deed. (It's interesting that in the Hebrew, this 'religious' question can also be interpreted as a political one: 'What can I do to cover up what happened?') Being a true political pragmatist, David turns over seven of Saul's descendants, whom the Gibeonites take out and hang. And then, to add further insult, the bodies are left out in the open for the birds to feast on.

But, like Antigone with her brother, the mother of two of the hanged men will not let the bodies of her sons and their kinsmen be treated in such a manner. Rizpah takes sackcloth, spreads it on a rock, and spends six months (!) watching over the bodies, not allowing the birds of the air or the scavenging wild beasts to get at them.

Against all the odds, this woman, this concubine, this outsider, breaks the cycle of retribution and revenge. Her protection of the bodies and her outpouring of love shames David to act. He not only buries the seven men he had given over to the Gibeonites, but brings home the bones of Saul and Jonathan and inters them with honour.

First Thursday of Advent

And the famine is broken! God heeds the prayers of the people not because of what David had done, but by the simple act, the profound sacrifice, of Rizpah, who taught David that retribution and revenge are not the answer. By her refusing to become a participant in revenge, David sees what he has become, and is transformed into a person of sympathy and compassion.

Where are the Rizpahs in our time, in our world, in our brokenness, in our continual desire for retribution and revenge?

Prayer

Raise up the Rizpahs we need, Broken-hearted God, that brokenness might be made whole, that peace and justice might reign in all peoples and lands, that compassion and hope might be what we offer to those who have hurt us. In Jesus' name, we pray. Amen

DANCE! DANCE! DANCE!

Read Exodus 15:20–21

There's not enough celebration in the Church; there's not enough rejoicing; there's not enough dancing. Maybe that's why I like Miriam.

Her name means 'bitter', for she was born in the time of the greatest oppression of the Hebrew people in Egypt. There was no future for God's people – no hope waiting for them just around the corner, no liberating army marching to rescue them. But in this time of great despair, the Talmud says, a young girl, Miriam, prophesied: 'My mother will give birth to a son who will redeem Israel.' And you can imagine the reaction of the people to such an utterance.

But Miriam remained faithful, believing that the promise God had given her would be fulfilled. She believed it when her little brother Moses was born. She kept faith when he was placed in that basket and set afloat. She was an instrument of promise-keeping when she encouraged Pharaoh's daughter to use a Hebrew woman to nurse Moses, bringing in his natural mother for the job.

And she refused to be true to her name through the scandal of Moses' crimes and his escape; through the long years of his absence from Egypt; through all the nights and days of wondering if the promises made long ago would be kept. She trusted, and hoped, and endured. According to tradition, she was so hopeful that what she had prophesied would come true, she convinced the other Hebrew women to make tambourines – hardly a musical instrument for times of bitterness and pain – and to be ready for the day of liberation.

First Friday of Advent

And, finally, the promises came true. Moses returned, the people were led out of Egypt, and set on the path to freedom and new life in the Promised Land. And when they were on the path, this oldest child who was always in the shadow of her youngest brother, this young woman who was always eclipsed by her male siblings, this marvellous woman who was always known as 'Aaron's sister', leaves her bitterness on the far banks of the sea, grabs up her tambourine, and dances!

Prayer

Liberating God, as you come in this season of Advent to release us from our fears, our pain, our bitterness, our worries, may we leave them behind us and dance to the stable where we will meet our promised Redeemer, and joyfully embrace him. Amen

I LOVE MYSTERIES

Read Ecclesiastes 3:1–8

'I don't know. It's a mystery.'

This repeated line from the movie *Shakespeare in Love* is a favourite of mine. We are always searching for answers. My family lost everything it had in the Great Depression … Why? My best friend died in Vietnam, and I came through without a scratch … How? Small and inconsequential moments; tragic and never-ending calamities … Why is it God allows these things to happen? Sometimes all we can answer is: 'I don't know. It's a mystery.'

The writer of Ecclesiastes (also known as the Preacher and the Speaker) understood that there is a rhythm to life. There are seasons we live through, and some that almost overcome us. There are times we barely endure, and moments when we are able to achieve great success. There are those moments which lay us flat on our backs, and those times when we are able to lift others and put them back on their feet.

Why do unbearable, horrendous, shattering moments happen to some people all the time, while others of us seemingly glide through life without hitting a single pothole in the road? I don't know. It's a mystery. But what I do know is that even when our times seem out of joint with God's time, even when it seems that what we experience on Earth has nothing to do with what God intends for us, even when, from moment to moment, we wonder if we are in control of our lives, God is in control. It may, indeed, be a mystery we cannot solve, but in every moment, every time, every season we face, God gives us the mysterious gift of grace – precious moments of peace, pleasure, silence and contentment that help us to live through those difficult times.

First Saturday of Advent

Prayer

Creator of time, we are in a season of preparation, of hope, of expectation. For some of us, it is a time we see clearly and rejoice in every day. For others, the days are dim, cloudy, mysterious. Remind us that you are in control and, though we may not see you, you see us and hold us in your love. Amen

SECOND
WEEK

AMAZING UN-GRACE

Read Genesis 21:8–12

Ever wanted something so badly you could cry? I'm not talking about what you are hoping to find under the Christmas tree this year, but something so important, so vital to your personhood, yet so unattainable. Say, a child.

Sarah knew what it was like to dream: to dream of holding her own child; to dream of watching her baby grow through childhood, adolescence and adulthood; to dream of sharing in the tears and the laughter, the ups and downs. She knew what it was like to hope, and to yearn, and to wish beyond all imagining. And she knew the bitter reality that her dreams would never come true. She was too old, too barren, too filled with the nightmare of nothingness, rather than the full dreams of everything.

But for God, neither age, nor disease, nor circumstance, nor anything can stand in the way of fulfilling dreams. Not only the dreams of a person, but God's dreams for a people, a nation, a world. And so Sarah's dream comes true … and Isaac is born to her.

And what is her response?

This woman, whose dreams were fulfilled, dashes the dreams of another; this mother, who was given a son to love and cherish, turns spiteful and bitter towards Hagar's son; this child of God, who had been filled with grace, turns an ungracious back on Ishmael and Hagar, having them driven from their home and into the wilderness.

This is one of the truths about human beings revealed in scripture. Read the prophet of Advent, Isaiah. People who have been blessed with God's gifts withhold them from the poor. Those who have been brought out of slavery into

Second Sunday of Advent

freedom oppress their neighbours. The ones who had nothing but the clothes on their backs become wasteful users of the resources of all creation.

Only by God's gracious working in us can we change.

Prayer

This Advent, as we wait to celebrate grace incarnate in our lives, may we be more gracious – more forgiving, more accepting – to everyone we know and meet. In the name of Christ, we pray. Amen

SEALED LIPS

Read Luke 1:5–25

Here at church, the children are working on making Jesse trees. One of our creative folks has made a banner for each child, and the leader of the workshops has created marvellous symbols for each person in the Bible stories, which the children make and hang on their trees. As you might imagine, there is an apple for Adam and Eve, a rainbow for Noah, a harp for David, etc. But yesterday morning the leader mentioned that she was stumped on what symbol to create for Zechariah.

Seemed pretty obvious to me – a smiley face with a zipper where the mouth goes!

But she's right, it is hard to come up with a symbol for this player in the divine production that is taking place in the pages of scripture. And, if scripture is correct, it was hard to be someone named Zechariah.

2 Chronicles 24:20–23 tells of the priest Zechariah who was stoned to death for his unpopular preaching (a passage ministers might want to keep hidden from their flocks!); 2 Kings 15:8–12 recounts the story of King Zechariah who ruled for only six months before being assassinated; and then there is the 'little brother' prophet, who always stood in the shadow of Isaiah, Jeremiah and Ezekiel. And in today's reading, all Zechariah did was ask for a 'sign' – what proof is there of these promises being made to Elizabeth and me?

Maybe Zechariah was struck speechless so he didn't have to answer all the questions people would ask when they discovered that Elizabeth was pregnant. Maybe he was struck speechless because his doubts outweighed his faith. Maybe he was struck speechless so that, in the ensuing silence, he could hear

Second Monday of Advent

what it was that God had to say to him.

This season is so noisy, so jangling, so discordant; we are so busy chatting on the telephone, talking to sales clerks, trying to run down the best bargains; we are so busy asking for a sign of God's presence in our world that we can't hear the cries of the infants seeking our attention. We have become such a part of all the noise of this time that we can't hear the whispers of the angels.

Prayer

Holy God, for a season, for a day, for an hour, even for a moment, may we become speechless that your Word might shape our hearts and souls. Amen

LET THE CHILDREN LEAD US

Read Isaiah 11:1–10

Advent's prophet, Isaiah, offers us a vision of a time when enemies will sit down and talk with one another, when predators will take naps with their former prey, when carnivores will become vegetarians. And we read such words, and nod our heads as we smile and say to ourselves, 'Not a chance, Isaiah! We watch reality TV, and we know this is not the way the world operates.'

Is it only a fantasy, a utopian dream, a pie in the sky wish that will never be fulfilled? Seems like it, doesn't it? After all, our cat and dog can't even get along with one another, so how can we expect the cow and the bear and the lion and the calf to become willing playmates?

And we humans … Well, we all know how hard it is to let go of the hurt that someone has done to us; to be willing to lay down the grudge we have against that sibling from so many years ago. We all know how long we can hold on to the words our spouse hurled at us in anger, and how a perceived slight or an unfulfilled expectation can fester in a congregation.

Maybe we need to take Isaiah's words to heart, and let a child lead us. Certainly the Christ Child, but it could be any child. Watch kids at play. Things are going smoothly, and suddenly something happens, anger erupts, words fly about like leaves on an autumn afternoon; best friends tell one another they never want to see each other again as long as they live, as they stomp off home. And then a day, an hour, even a few minutes later, they are racing one another down to the playground, to laugh and play and care for one another for the rest of their lives.

Second Tuesday of Advent

The words have drifted away, the anger has melted into friendship, the grudges have been left behind as they grab hands and swing in circles.

Every day, we see God's kingdom, and Isaiah's vision of it, enacted before our eyes … if we only notice, and listen, and let the children lead us.

Prayer

The box would be pretty big and awfully heavy, Understanding God, but perhaps this year I will package up all my hurt, all my anger, all my grudges, and give them to you, that I might have enough room to receive your Child into my heart. In Advent hope, I pray. Amen

ONCE UPON A TIME ...

Read The Book of Ruth (or at least 1:1–5,17; 2:4–13; 3:1–5; 4:11–22)

'Once upon a time' is the way most of us remember stories from our child-hood. Stories that filled us with wonder (and sometimes fear), stories that taught us valuable lessons, stories that told us about people who would make good role models or mentors. I wonder if Jesus ever heard stories that began 'Once upon a time ...'

'Once upon a time we call sacred, in a land we call holy, there was a woman named Ruth ...'

'Do I know her, Mummy?'

'No, no, dear child. She was born long before you were, but she is a part of our family. She is your, let's see, great-great-great-great, well, I don't know how many 'greats' to put in front, but she was the great-grandmother of King David.'

'Wow. A very important person, a very famous Hebrew woman, wasn't she?'

'One would think that, but she was not Jewish. She was a native of the land of Moab. She married into a Jewish family who had moved to Moab during a terrible famine. But her husband died, and when her mother-in-law moved back to Bethlehem, Ruth went with her. There she looked after her mother-in-law, and gleaned in the fields for food. She met and ended up marrying a man from the tribe of Judah, named Boaz, and they started their family, which you were born into.'

'But Mummy, didn't the rabbi read from the Torah that no Moabite could marry into Israel for ten generations?'

Second Wednesday of Advent

'Ah, you listen too well sometimes, son. Yes, the Torah says that. But maybe it was all right, because Ruth was not, strictly speaking, a Moabite. That is, a man. She was a woman, a Moabitess. Perhaps that's why the elders did not object.'

'I see. But why is she so important? I mean, she got married and had a child. That happens all the time.'

'Yes, son, that's true. But remember, she was an outsider who became a part of the Chosen; she was a woman who was willing to challenge the injustices of her time; she was a poor person who endured through terrible struggles; a widow herself, she had great compassion for another widow, her mother-in-law Naomi. Her Hebrew name means to 'fill' or 'replenish'. I think she refreshed a lot of people, including our family, with the ways she was obedient to God.'

'She certainly did things differently than most people expected. I wonder if I would be as willing to do things differently.'

Prayer

A famine of the spirit can be just as hard as physical hunger. Challenging God, fill our hearts with examples of people like Ruth; folks who are willing to take risks, to be compassionate, to step forth in faith, to follow you wherever you may lead them. In Jesus' name, we pray. Amen

THE ONE YOU LEAST EXPECT

Read Isaiah 45:1–7

You have fallen into a terrible predicament. It might be a physical disaster, it might be a financial reversal, it might be a severe emotional problem. In the midst of this calamity, you think about who it is that will be able to help you – family, friends, co-workers. Quick – name the person who is going to come to your rescue. Can you see them in your mind's eye; can you hear his or her voice speaking to you; can you almost reach out and touch them?

Now, think about that one person who, for whatever reason, would never, ever, even if you gave them everything you had on earth, come to your aid. It might be that friend you had a falling out with years ago; it might be the boss who threw you out the door; it might be the spouse who walked out on you.

Then imagine you discover that this is the person God is using to deliver you. Not your shining knight riding in on a white horse; not your best friend who has stood by you through thick and thin; not your mother who has always pulled you out of every hole you have dug for yourself – but an antagonist, an outsider, a stranger.

That's the surprise Isaiah announces in this passage. The people are eagerly awaiting the one whom God is sending to bring them out of exile, to lead them on that journey back to Jerusalem, to be in the front of that pack of people who are ready to go home – singing, clapping, dancing all the way. The trembling throng whispers, 'Has anyone heard who it is yet? Maybe it is Isaiah himself who is coming? Maybe one of David's descendants?'

Then the shocking revelation: It is not the king they hoped for, not the wordsmith they wanted to hear, not a prophet calling them to task. Of all the

39

Second Thursday of Advent

people in the world God could have chosen, God chooses a Gentile – Cyrus. And not only that, God calls this foreigner the Messiah, God's anointed.

Another unexpected move by the One who continues to refuse to be boxed in by our expectations, who will not be bound by past deeds, who will not be limited to doing things the way they have always been done. The One who is the author of all is always in the process of writing new chapters for God's people.

Prayer

God, we expect you to be the same, act the same, speak the same. So, as we expect this Advent and Christmas to be the same as all the others we have experienced in the past, nudge us, just a little, to be prepared for the surprises you might have in store for us this season. This we pray in the name of Jesus, the Messiah, the Prince of Peace. Amen

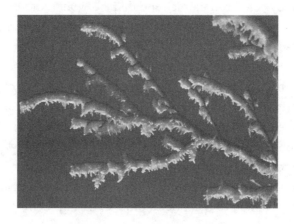

PLANTING SEEDS

Read Esther 5:1–8

For some people, the stories of the people in the Bible are like seeds that are planted deep within them the first time they hear them. They are watered and nourished with each new telling and receive warmth when people begin to take them to heart.

How many people have had the seed of the story of Esther planted within them at some point in their lives? This story of a woman who had everything and was willing to let it all go, and not just to save her cousin. Think how incredibly courageous an act it was for Esther to appear before the king. It went completely against every custom and set in motion the events which saved a people.

Now think about all the people throughout the generations and centuries who heard this story and had that seed of courage planted within them.

Dietrich Bonhoeffer maybe. What great courage it took him to return to his native Germany when it was faced with the evil of Nazism. A gifted pastor, a brilliant theologian, a consummate preacher – maybe the seed of Esther blossomed in him at that time.

And Rosa Parks? I'll bet she heard this story in church when she was growing up, this story of a woman who was violating all the customs of her time, who was willing to stand before the powerful and influential and to work for change. Maybe the seed of Esther which was planted in Rosa when she was a child finally burst forth that day on the bus in Montgomery, Alabama.

Who's to know, who's to say? But I have seen the seed of Esther planted in people I know very well, and I give thanks that they have nurtured that seed, and allowed it to blossom in their lives.

Second Friday of Advent

Prayer

Gardener of Creation, continue to plant seeds deep within us; water them with living waters; nourish them with the stories of people just like us; warm them with your Son; and help us to be the good soil in which they can grow and bloom. In thanks for Esther and all the people who have followed her example, we pray. Amen

PRECIOUS TREASURE

Read Genesis 33:1–17

One of the first clues in scripture that God does not operate the way humans expect or want God to act is how the eldest son is treated in the stories found in Genesis. In a time and culture in which the oldest male received everything – privilege, wealth, land, blessing – we discover that it may not be the best position in the household of faith God is creating.

Take Esau, for instance. Whether through his own foolishness, or through the deception of his younger brother (encouraged by Mum), Esau loses his status as the most important child in the family. Instead of being the conduit of the promises given to his grandparents and parents, he sees Jacob become the favoured one, the blessed one, the golden one.

Yet, despite what has happened to him and being tricked out of everything held most dear to him, Esau forgives Jacob. Esau could have clung to bitterness, but did not. He could have taken revenge, but refused. He could have turned on his younger brother and have done to him what Cain did to Abel, but he chooses another path.

And when Jacob returns home, after his journeys to Aram, Esau runs to meet his brother and embraces him, weeping and kissing him as if Jacob is now his most precious treasure, no longer his most bitter memory. The one who was hurt the most lets go of that burden that he might sweep his brother up into his arms.

What a story, what a person, what a model to pass on to succeeding generations, who would tell of this gracious and reconciling act. No wonder the author of Hebrews writes that Esau is a bearer of blessings (Heb 11:20).

Second Saturday of Advent

And no wonder that perhaps the most intimate parable that Jesus tells is a story about a prodigal, younger son who returns home and is met by the one person he has hurt the most, and who, instead of rejecting him, runs to his son and embraces him and sweeps him up in his arms, never to let go.

Prayer

Gracious God, we are more than willing to run and pick up the sweet and innocent Child lying in the manger. Make us just as eager to embrace those who have shoved us away, to kiss those who have brushed us off, to hold and love and care for those who have washed their hands of us. In Jesus' name, we pray. Amen

THIRD
WEEK

ARE YOU THE ONE?

Read Matthew 11:2–11

A cool cloth
laid gently on
a fevered brow;

holding hands with
a parkinsoned grandmother;

singing carols
with a father
who cannot remember his name:

hope
is the comfort
we give to others.

As we grieve
the loss of wisdom
in the ones
who taught us so much;

as we work to transform
a culture which marginalises
the aged, the battered, the 'limited';

Third Sunday of Advent

as we serve those
who have
no food,
no shelter,
no joy,

hope
is the protest
we cry out to heaven.

Are you the One
we hope for?

Come, Lord Jesus,
hope of all hearts.
Come.
Amen

SHE IS STILL AMONG US

Read 2 Samuel 11:1–21, 26

Some say that Bathsheba brought these events upon herself. But David is the one who summons her into his royal presence.

Some say that she bathed out on the patio of her home, knowing the king's terrace looked down upon it. But the law allowed for the ritual bath of purification to be done in her own vicinity.

Some say the story is told to reveal the weaknesses of David, and to set in motion the violence, the intrigue, the rivalries for his throne. But Bathsheba is a part of this story not because she is weak, but because she is powerless.

She is powerless because she is a woman, and has no rights of her own. She has no power because she is married to an officer in David's army, and cannot risk his career. She is powerless because how can one person stand up against the authority, the commands, the demands of God's king? The final statement about her powerlessness is made in Matthew's genealogy of Jesus, when he speaks of her not by name, but only as 'the wife of Uriah'. (Matt 1:6b)

Yet, she is the ancestress of the One who gives up all his power in order to come and serve us. She is the forebear of the Christ who lets go of all the might in creation in order to kneel at our feet and wash them. She is the relative of the anointed of God who calls each of us his sister or brother. She is of the house of the Messiah who comes to lead us into the kingdom of God, where we live in peace and reconciliation with one another.

Bathsheba is still among us: powerless, voiceless. She is the single mother who must choose between food and medicine for her sick child. She is the immigrant who seeks political asylum from terror. She is the father who works

Third Monday of Advent

three jobs so that his children can go to college and have a better life. She is the 340 million children in Africa who are forced to scrabble for mere existence. She is the family who sleep under the bridges of the roads we drive over on our way to and from work. She is the mentally challenged young man sitting on death row, not understanding why.

And she is the one we are called to serve in this season of waiting to celebrate the coming of the Christ Child and the return of our Lord and Saviour.

Prayer

Holy God of Bethlehem and Bathsheba, we may not consider ourselves to be powerful people like kings or politicians, but each of us has the power to help change the life of another person, by our compassion, by our generosity, by our forgiveness, by our love. Empower us to do so, we pray. Amen

WHEN I WAS EIGHT

Read 2 Kings 22:1b,10–11; 23:1–3

When I was eight years old, I was 'King of the Wild Frontier', imagining I was Davy Crockett, proudly wearing my (fake) raccoon-skin cap (just like millions of other kids). When he was eight years old, Josiah was made King of Judah, following the assassination of his father, King Amon. Big difference in responsibilities, huh?

By the time he was 26, Josiah had brought about the restoration of the temple, beginning a period of religious reform that was much needed by the people. Sparking this reform was the discovery of the Book of the Covenant (or law) in some of the rubble that was being removed from the temple.

This book, which we call the Book of Deuteronomy, led to a period of spiritual renewal that was unprecedented in Judah's history. Cast as three addresses, or sermons, given by Moses before the people crossed into the Promised Land, it is a reinterpretation of the covenant at Sinai to be relevant to the people of Josiah's time. By making a covenant with God again (2 Kings 23:3), Josiah and the people are once again stating their intention to be in partnership with God, to be obedient to God's call to faithful living.

Maybe Josiah was able to do all this because of his youth, I don't know. It seems that younger people often have a clearer view of things. They aren't as locked into the past, into traditions, into the 'way it has always been done'. They are much more open to the mystery, the wonder, the presence of God.

I wonder what sort of spiritual reforms would take place if we involved our young people more, rather than asking them to wait until they are 'older and wiser'. I wonder what sort of rebuilding would take place in our churches if we

Third Tuesday of Advent

paid more personal attention to children and young people, rather than just handing them over to the few folks who are willing to teach them in Sunday school. I wonder what our churches would be like if we were as willing to welcome children and youth as eagerly as we seem to want to welcome the Christ Child each year at this time.

I wonder ...

Prayer

Open our hearts to the children and youth in our lives and churches, Ever-young God, that we may learn from them, and be more like them: alert, caring, alive, committed. Hear us as we pray. Amen

THE SERVANT

Read Isaiah 50:4–9a

He's not listed in either Matthew's or Luke's genealogy of Jesus, but there may not be a more profound influence on the life of our Lord than the servant sung about by the prophet Isaiah. While the fourth servant song, Isaiah 52:12–53:12 (always read on Good Friday), is probably more familiar to most of us, this third song is the one that speaks most intimately about the relationship between the servant and the One who has called.

God is the One who has taught the servant, giving him the words which are to be spoken. And not just any words, but words which will speak to people who have been beaten down by life. The Word become flesh who dwells among us gives *us* such words ... Do we share them at the right moments with the people we know and meet?

God is the helper who opens the ears of the servant to hear the divine words. By listening to God, the servant knows whom he is called to serve; by listening to the needs of others, he discovers the gifts he has to use; by discovering his gifts, the servant knows who has gifted him and called him. In this season of Advent, are we listening as intently to God as we are to the songs on the radio?

Speaking God's word, daring to live out God's call, being willing to reach out and minister to the children of God marginalised by society, the servant will endure not only the 'slings and arrows' of the world but the ridicule and rejection of those he seeks to serve and, if necessary, physical pain as well. But the servant knows that God has not just given him a task and then gone back into the office and shut the door. God will defend the servant from all attacks

Third Wednesday of Advent

and will heal all the wounds the servant incurs on our behalf.

The servant serves as a model for the faithful who, in every time and place, are called to incarnate God's presence: to console the burdened, to heal the broken-hearted, to stand alongside those who are on the sidelines of society, to defend those who are willing to demand justice for the oppressed of our world.

How are you being called by the Christ Child to serve?

Prayer

Open our ears, Servant God, that we hear your voice; open our eyes, that we see the weariness of your children; open our mouths, that we offer words of hope; open our hearts, that we serve in your name. Amen

TRY TO REMEMBER

Read Hosea 11:1–11

Do you remember

- holding your newborn to your face, and feeling their sweet, innocent breath on your cheek;
- walking your child in the middle of the night when they just couldn't sleep;
- trying not to laugh as they wobbled precariously,
  getting up the courage to let go of the table leg
  and try that first, faltering step;
- holding your breath as she went down the sidewalk,
  peddling furiously on the bicycle without training wheels;
- building a tent in your living room with blankets and furniture,
  because you promised your nephews a camp-out,
  and the storm is not letting up;
- lying awake at 12, or 1, or whatever, in the middle of the night,
  waiting to hear the key in the lock
  telling you he's home from his date;
  do you remember?
  Of course you do!

Which is why you overlook the piles of dirty laundry, books, CDs and musical instruments that are growing in the bedroom; why you forgive her that she does not write every week from college; why you welcome them home when the job, or marriage, or dream is gone; why you still lie awake in the middle of the night worrying about them, so far away, so hard to take care of, so fragile and vulnerable still.

God remembers.

God remembers teaching us to walk,
    and watching us run away in rebellion.
God remembers taking us up in the arms of love,
    even as we screamed to have our own way.
God remembers feeding us in the wilderness,
    even though we swore we had been led there to starve to death.
God remembers ...

which is why Jesus comes:

to pick us up when we have fallen,
    and to brush the sin of the world off us;
to reach out and pull us back onto the Holy Way,
    which winds through the world to the kingdom;
to stretch his arms out on the cross
    to embrace us with new life;
to be wrapped in strips of cloth, and laid in a cold tomb,
    so that death is left behind when he is risen.

God remembers.

Do you?

Prayer

Please don't forget us, Precious God, please don't forget us – ever. Amen

AT THE LAST MINUTE

Read Micah 6:1–8

Okay, confession time. I am one of those people who wait until the last minute to get their Christmas presents bought. It would be nice to blame it on the fact that ministry, especially at this time of year, is very hectic, and there are not enough hours in the day. But truth be known, I have always been this way. Before I became a minister, I used to go shopping on Christmas Eve!

I am always scrambling around at the last minute trying to find the right gifts for the special people in my life. If I had been the fourth magi, it would have been too bad for baby Jesus. Along with the gold, myrrh and frankincense, he would have got whatever was left on the shelf at the only store open in downtown Bethlehem.

I think part of my resistance to shopping early is that I never really know what to get folks. Oh, they give me lists, but, if they are like me, their lists were made only because someone asked for them. I am fortunate enough to be able to buy whatever I really need, and so are most of my friends and family. Don't get me wrong, I enjoy giving 'things' to my friends and family, especially to my nieces and nephews, but these gifts are never really anything crucial to their life development.

So, what could I give my friends and family this year that might have some meaning? What would I give to baby Jesus if I had the chance? What could I give back to God?

Micah suggests that a marvellous gift would be to act justly. I don't think this necessarily means to obey the traffic lights and other laws, though those are important. But it certainly means to make sure that my friends and family

Third Friday of Advent

and my neighbours and colleagues are treated fairly. It certainly means that I act so that those who have no justice receive it – that those who have no voice have an advocate, that those who are treated cruelly are given a fair shake.

Micah tells me that another gift I could give to others is loving-kindness. While I am certainly kind to little kids, to stray animals, and to little old ladies needing help getting across the street (I do remember some things from the Boy Scouts!), I need to go a little deeper and to offer that unconditional love in every moment and in every encounter to every person, just as God offers it to me.

And while I certainly need to walk more for my health and to get rid of those spare tyres I carry around with me, I would like to walk more with God. Not in an arrogant way, like I know all the answers and have no doubts or fears, but in a way that shows folks that the only reason I can put one foot in front of another is because I have a God who wants to walk with me through life. A God who not only walks with me, but waits patiently for me to catch up whenever I stop because the road seems too long or too difficult.

I don't believe I will find any of these gifts at the mall – even if I had done my shopping back in the summer. But I know where I *will* find them, even at the last minute.

Prayer

Help me to deal justly with others, Kind God, as you deal with me. May I love others as openly and trustingly and completely as you do, Just God. And may I always seek to walk with you, Pilgrim God.

MAKING THE RIGHT CHOICE

Read 1 Kings 3:5–9 and Matthew 4:1–11

When I am on a diet, I don't need the Evil One to tempt me. Every fast food joint I drive past, every crisp bag in the store, every candy bar at the checkout line sings its siren call to me. And, if you know me well, you know the choice I make all too often.

Still, while I have no real desire to run for any political office, I am convinced that I could make better choices than most of the people on the City Council of my home town, Cincinnati – that a lot of the time I could do a better job than just about every politician I read about in the paper, no matter what their office!

So, how did Jesus do it? How was he able to reject the temptations offered to him out there in the wilderness? How did he keep from jumping at the chance to have his 40-day-old hunger alleviated, or to have his physical pain healed, or to have more power than Herod, Pilate and the latest Caesar put together?

The only answer I can come up with is that, given the chance for anything in the world, Jesus instead opted for wisdom, like his ancestor Solomon. Wise enough to choose between good and evil, Jesus knew who it was who sustained him in the wilderness. Wise enough to turn his back on the Evil One, Jesus went forth to serve God's people. Wise enough to know where following every whim, every need, every hunger would lead him, Jesus chose to be obedient to God, even when that choice was the more difficult one.

Third Saturday of Advent

Prayer

Wisdom Incarnate, in the birth of the Christ Child, which we will celebrate in one week, you have kept the greatest promise of all. Make us wise enough to trust that promise and that fulfilment, that we are always obedient in our call. In Jesus' name, we pray. Amen

FOURTH WEEK

THE LONGEST NIGHT

Read Matthew 1:18–25

Tonight we will be hosting our annual 'Longest Night Service' at the church. Called 'Blue Christmas' in some communities, it is a respite offered to those for whom this season is not holy but lonely; to those whose times are not filled with joy, but with grief; to those whose homes are not filled with family and friends, but with the empty ache of loss.

This is the ninth consecutive year we have offered this special service. If truth be told, it probably grew out of the chronic grief I have experienced over the situation with our son: the recognition that his brokenness will only be made whole in God's future; that the pain I carry around in my heart will be a lifelong companion.

It is obvious from the response each year that this is a service that speaks to many people in a very genuine and needed way. Many of the same folks return. And many new people come. As I set up the sanctuary for the service this afternoon, I wondered, Will Joseph be here tonight?

I can imagine the feeling of loss Joseph must have experienced when he heard that Mary was pregnant. He must have sensed that any respect his family and friends had for him had vanished. As he wandered the village streets, he must have wondered how many people were whispering about him or laughing behind their doors.

The dreams he had harboured all his life about marriage, about life with Mary, about starting a family, were now nightmares, as his family pressured him to dump the woman he loved with all his heart or demanded the ultimate punishment for her.

Fourth Sunday of Advent

The doubts he entertained were worse than any physical torment that Mary could have inflicted on him. Was her story true, this wild tale about an angel? Could he believe the dream that had danced in his mind the other night, or was that just the sour wine he'd drunk in his despair? Was he really a part of that prophecy the rabbi was always quoting from the Book of Isaiah?

The loss of a loved one, a job, a dream; broken promises and shattered relationships; doubts about the future and nightmares from our pasts – all reasons why people come to our Longest Night Service. All reasons why we offer this sacred space and this holy moment – for ourselves, for friends, for strangers, for all the Josephs among us.

Prayer

He might have passed me on the street today, as I walked the dog. She might have been the neighbour with few decorations on her house, or the child with his eyes widening at all the toys in the store, but none in his hands. Broken people, lonely people, hopeless people, your people, Broken-hearted God. Heal us in this season of hope and promises, Tender God, as you have promised. Amen

SO FRAYED, SO FRAZZLED

Read Isaiah 40:3–11

So frayed, so frazzled,
so harried, so hassled ...

It's so hard to get prepared:
just when we think every present is bought,
an unexpected one arrives,
and, of course, we have to go out
and buy one for that person;
as we gaze at the outside lights
that have been hung and arranged
so lovingly and carefully,
a strand goes out,
and there is another trip to the store.

We know the way to the mall so well
we could drive there with our eyes closed
(and almost do sometimes!);
the path to the post office is well-worn
from all the trips to mail packages
and get more stamps.

Christmas Day draws nearer and nearer
and the activity level increases
(as does our stress);
the days grow shorter and shorter

Fourth Monday of Advent

(since we obviously don't have
enough hours in each one
to get everything done).

So frayed, so frazzled,
so harried, so hassled …

We might not hear the voice calling to us:
'Prepare the way, the Lord is coming;
God's path will lead you straight to the kingdom.'
Open our ears, Lord, open our ears.
Amen

TOO TIRED TO SLEEP

Read Luke 2:1–7

I didn't think I would have so much trouble falling asleep. After all, we are all exhausted: so many folks clamouring for food, for wine, for a place to stay. This registration thing the Roman ruler called for has turned out to be a real financial bonanza for everyone I know.

Maybe I'm too tired to sleep, too wound up from all the hustle and bustle of the last few days. I knew that we expected big crowds, but I never knew there were so many people who could trace themselves back to King David, may his name be preserved for ever! Not bad for a guy who started out as nothing more than a shepherd.

Or it could be that star that has been shining so much over the last few weeks. It just keeps getting brighter and brighter. The Jeremiahs among us are whispering that it is heading straight for Jerusalem, so we had all better get our affairs in order; but really – it's just a big, bright star! Though the light does come through the curtains at night as if they are not even there.

I just wish I could get some rest. I've worked hard, I've played hard, I've drunk enough wine to put a camel on its hump, but sleep just keeps slipping out of my fingers whenever I try to grasp hold of it.

And no, I don't think it's my conscience that is keeping me awake, thank you very much. A businessman has to make tough choices. And if someone comes in offering you triple the room rate you've already doubled because of the crowds, well, some folks lose out … even family. And, after all, it's not as if they are *real* family. Just some sort of fourth or fifth cousins from way up north, come to town for the registration, who don't have two denarii to rub together.

Fourth Tuesday of Advent

Sure, normally I would give them the room I always hold back for unexpected guests, but that unexpected sack of gold that the family from Tyre offered me was a little more convincing.

Besides, even if they are family, I don't have to countenance the kind of lifestyle they lead. Oh yeah, even down here in Bethlehem word has reached us about Mary and her 'difficulty'. None of us can understand why Joseph didn't do the right thing and get rid of her (one way or another, if you catch my drift). I mean, we are a people of family values, aren't we? Even if they are family, they don't get an excuse for how they behave. I mean, I would kick my own daughter out of the house if she came home with a ridiculous story like Mary's. We do have to stick to our principles when life gets sticky, don't we? Isn't that what the Lord requires of us?

But, I do wish I could get some sleep.

Prayer

We would hope, God, that family would come before 'values', that justice would come instead of judgement, that love would trump legalism. We can hope, can't we? In Jesus' name, we pray. Amen

A FLAWED LEADER

Read 2 Samuel 12:1–7a

I am an unabashed fan of the TV show *The West Wing* here in the United States. For those of you who are not familiar with the show, it is about the White House of a fictional President Bartlett. While it is TV, it does provide some of us with a glimpse of a president we wish we had and of the way White House staff should function.

One of the things I like about the programme is that it is willing to show the characters in all their humanness – with all their flaws and foibles, all their arrogance, all their passions, all their self-righteousness, as well as with all their good qualities, like their strong loyalty to the person in the Oval Office. It shows a president who makes mistakes and unwise decisions; and a president who faces his mistakes and unwise decisions and deals with the consequences. Whether it is dealing with the repercussions of not revealing to the American people that he has multiple sclerosis or with the fall-out from the assassination of a foreign leader, President Bartlett is shown to be all too human.

This is a good quality to see in politicians, in my humble opinion. It not only makes them more humble but also makes them better 'servant leaders'.

I well remember, as a kid in Sunday school, hearing the stories about all the women and men in the Bible and thinking, *Wow! David was someone special, someone who never made mistakes, someone who did everything exactly the way God wanted him to do things. What a role model!*, knowing all the while that I could never match his faith, his commitment, his singular focus on serving God. I mean, he slays a giant, goes from shepherd to special assistant to the king, marries the king's daughter, and then becomes king.

Then, one Sunday, the preacher read this passage from 2nd Samuel. Wait a minute! David made a mistake – and not just a mistake but one with a capital M. He did something that had repercussions on his life, on the life of Uriah, on the people of Israel, on his family and on his relationship with God. This is the role model that church had held up to me for years?!

But, like Leo McGarry who is always willing to confront President Bartlett (as well as encourage him), David had Nathan calling him to account, reminding him that, as a leader and as a follower of God, he should have higher standards.

And the good news is that David was willing to be confronted; David was willing to be held accountable; David was more committed to his relationship with God than he was to public opinion. David was willing to face his sin, to repent of it, and to let God's redemption of his actions change his life. And, in doing so, he became a more effective shepherd of God's people, more a servant than a leader. Now that's not a bad role model!

Prayer

I slide my feet of clay into my shoes every day, Redeeming God, knowing how frail and fallible I am in my struggle to be your child, to be your servant. Help me not to worry so much about my prestige, but about the possibilities to share your good news with others each day. May I always be willing to confess my failings to you, that you might redeem them and use them in the work of your kingdom. In the name of your servant, Jesus Christ, I pray. Amen

THE RADICAL FAMILY LINE

Read Genesis 38:1–30

I remember the first time it struck me how radical it seemed for Matthew to include women in the genealogy of Jesus. In that era, women were property; women were lower than whatever class was lowest; women had no standing, no power, no voice, no anything. Yet, here they are – Rahab, the heroine of a gutsy spy novel; Ruth, the epitome of Old Testament loyalty and perseverance; and Bathsheba, misused by one with great power.

But Tamar? What do we do with Tamar? It's a story that makes us uncomfortable to read (why else is it not in any lectionary cycle of the church?) and difficult to preach on (the collection of great sermons on Tamar is still at the publishers, I guess). True, the levirate obligation involved in the story is difficult to explain. But the basic reason we are so uncomfortable reading (and preaching) this story is because we see it as a story about lust and sex and, even in 2005, we don't think 'stories like that' should be in the Bible.

But look beyond the ancient obligation, look beyond the so-called use of feminine 'wiles', look beyond the lust of Judah, and what do we discover? Not a story about unbridled passion, but a tale about a woman passionate in her quest for justice. It's not a story about a broken law, but a story about a woman who seeks to have the law fulfilled justly. It's not really a story about lust and sex, but a story about a family that has lost its way.

It began a few chapters earlier in Genesis, when older brother Judah pushes to have his younger brother, Joseph, sold into slavery. We aren't told all the details but, after this event, Judah leaves home and ends up marrying a Canaanite woman, and naming their children with Canaanite names. It is as if,

Fourth Thursday of Advent

in the act of injustice to Joseph, Judah has turned his back on his family, his culture, his faith.

It is obvious that if God's purposes are to be fulfilled, it will take someone else a little more obedient, a little more faithful than Judah. And so Tamar, like another woman generations later, is willing to face public ridicule and even the possibility of death in order for justice to take place.

And while her son Perez becomes part of the lineage that leads to David, and on to Jesus, of greater importance is the realisation that justice becomes a part of the family tree. Later in the book, Judah is willing to give his own life for the safety of Benjamin. And Jesus, heir of Tamar, becomes the one whose passion for justice leads him to break religious laws and social customs in order to serve others – to eat and drink with the rejected; to lift up women from the pit into which society had cast them and to make them an integral part of his ministry and of God's kingdom.

Prayer

Rather than turning our backs on her, Just God, let us invite Tamar to our Christmas feast, that we might learn a passion for justice which eludes us, that we might open our hearts to those cast out by our world, that we might break bread with one who restored her family to wholeness. In Jesus' name, we pray. Amen

IN SILENCE

In silence
you watched,
waited,
yearned,

until your heart
could break no more.

So you came to us
in a stable
where no one noticed you;
by a well
where you welcomed the outsider;
on a hillside
where you fed the hungry;
on a cross
where you died for us:

in love,
you came to us.

In silence
we watch,
wait,
yearn.

Come, Lord Jesus,
that we might rejoice once again. Amen

CHRISTMAS EVE

Read Luke 2:1–20

Sing! Sing! Sing!

Sing, choirs of angels!

for this is the night:

when our peace comes
not as a prince
but as a pauper;

when God reaches down
to wrap creation
in ribbons of love
and to place it in the kingdom;

when God holds us
to her breast
and feeds us
everlasting life;
when God lets go
of might
in order
to embrace
the marginalised;

Christmas Eve

when a baby gurgles
our name,
laughing and reaching out
to grab our hands
with his,
never to let go.

Through sin,
through denial,
through rejection,
through the hell
of death.
This is the night.

Sing!

CHRISTMAS DAY

This is the day
when we gather to celebrate:

some of us
on hard wooden pews
in sanctuaries
we have not haunted
for a very long time;

some of us
travelling long distances
physically
and emotionally
to be with people
who haunt us from our past;

some of us
around tables
with family and friends
who love us
despite our present.

And in the pew next to us
sit Esther and Achim,

and across the aisle
on the train
ride

Christmas Day

Bathsheba and David,

and setting the food on the table
is Sarah,

and saying the grace
for all of us
is Zechariah –

our ancestors,
our relatives,
our faith-bearers,
our Jesse tree:

our past
our present
our future

all secured by our God.

BLESSING

The trust of Abraham
  strengthen you;
the hospitality of Rahab
  enfold you;
the vision of Isaiah
  seize you;
the laughter of Sarah
  surprise you;
the dream of Micah
  awaken you;
the justice of Rizpah
  nudge you;

and may the living branch
of the Jesse tree bless and keep you
now and for ever. Amen

PHOTO CREDITS

.

THE IONA COMMUNITY IS:

- An ecumenical movement of men and women from different walks of life and different traditions in the Christian church
- Committed to the gospel of Jesus Christ, and to following where that leads, even into the unknown
- Engaged together, and with people of goodwill across the world, in acting, reflecting and praying for justice, peace and the integrity of creation
- Convinced that the inclusive community we seek must be embodied in the community we practise

Together with our staff, we are responsible for:

- Our islands residential centres of Iona Abbey, the MacLeod Centre on Iona, and Camas Adventure Centre on the Ross of Mull

and in Glasgow:

- The administration of the Community
- Our work with young people
- Our publishing house, Wild Goose Publications
- Our association in the revitalising of worship with the Wild Goose Resource Group

The Iona Community was founded in Glasgow in 1938 by George MacLeod, minister, visionary and prophetic witness for peace, in the context of the poverty and despair of the Depression. Its original task of rebuilding the monastic ruins of Iona Abbey became a sign of hopeful rebuilding of community in Scotland and beyond. Today, we are about 250 Members, mostly in Britain, and 1500 Associate Members, with 1400 Friends worldwide. Together and apart, 'we follow the light we have, and pray for more light'.

For information on the Iona Community contact:
The Iona Community, Fourth Floor, Savoy House, 140 Sauchiehall Street,
Glasgow G2 3DH, UK. Phone: 0141 332 6343
e-mail: ionacomm@gla.iona.org.uk; web: www.iona.org.uk

For enquiries about visiting Iona, please contact:
Iona Abbey, Isle of Iona, Argyll PA76 6SN, UK. Phone: 01681 700404
e-mail: ionacomm@iona.org.uk

ALSO FROM WILD GOOSE PUBLICATIONS ...

MORE RESOURCES FOR ADVENT & CHRISTMAS:

Candles & Conifers
Resources for All Saints' to Advent
Ruth Burgess

A collection of seasonal resources for groups and individuals – prayers, liturgies, poems, reflections, sermons, meditations, stories and responses, written by Iona Community members, associates, friends and others.

It covers the weeks from All Saints' Day to Christmas Eve, including saints' days, Remembrance Day, World AIDS Day and Advent. There are liturgies for an outdoor celebration with fireworks, a Christingle service and a longest night service, as well as Advent candle ceremonies, personal prayer practices, a series of responses and blessings and a cats' Advent calendar.

ISBN 1 901557 96 0

Hay & Stardust
Resources for Christmas to Candlemas
Ruth Burgess

This companion resource book to *Candles & Conifers* covers the season of Christmastide, including Christmas Eve, Holy Innocents' Day, Winter and New Year, Epiphany, Homelessness Sunday and Candlemas. It also contains eight Christmas plays, including a puppet play.

ISBN 1 905010 00 1

WWW.IONABOOKS.COM

Hear My Cry
A daily prayer book for Advent
Ruth Burgess

A daily prayer book for Advent which can also be used as a prayer journal, taking its inspiration from the Advent antiphons – a group of prayers that reflect on the character and activities of God. The format for each day includes a Bible verse, an Advent cry and suggestions for prayer. The pages can be added to and personalised, with line drawings that can be coloured in and space to add your own pictures, reflections and prayers. Instructions for three workshops are also included to enable Advent themes to be explored in a group setting.

ISBN 1 901557 95 2

Cloth for the Cradle
Worship resources & readings for Advent, Christmas and Epiphany
Wild Goose Worship Group

This rediscovery of the stories of Christ's birth through adult eyes contains much to reflect on individually and to use in group and worship situations. The material is drawn from the work of the Wild Goose Resource and Worship Groups whose innovative style of worship is widely admired and imitated.

SBN 1 901557 01 4

ALSO FROM WILD GOOSE PUBLICATIONS ...

MORE RESOURCES FOR ADVENT & CHRISTMAS:

Innkeepers and Light Sleepers
Seventeen new songs for Christmas   Songbook/CD
John L Bell

My bonnie boy • He became poor • Christmas is coming • Carol of the Advent • No wind at the window • Justice in the womb • And did it happen • Look up and wonder • God immersed in mystery • Funny kind of night • The pedigree • Ma wee bit dearie • Ho ro ho ro • The aye carol • Simeon's song • Carol of the Epiphany • The refugees

Songbook ISBN 0 947988 47 5
Cassette ISBN 0 947988 54 8
CD ISBN 1 901557 39 1

Advent Readings from Iona
Brian Woodcock & Jan Sutch Pickard

Celebrate Christmas with reflections and prayers for each day of Advent. This effective antidote to the commercialism of the festive season can be used for individual meditation or group worship. The authors are the former wardens of the Abbey on the Isle of Iona.

ISBN 1 905010 33 2

Wild Goose Publications, the publishing house of the Iona Community established in the Celtic Christian tradition of Saint Columba, produces books, tapes and CDs on:

- holistic spirituality
- social justice
- political and peace issues
- healing
- innovative approaches to worship
- song in worship, including the work of the Wild Goose Resource Group
- material for meditation and reflection

If you would like to find out more about our books, tapes and CDs, please contact us at:

Wild Goose Publications
Fourth Floor, Savoy House
140 Sauchiehall Street,
Glasgow G2 3DH, UK

Tel. +44 (0)141 332 6292
Fax +44 (0)141 332 1090
e-mail: admin@ionabooks.com

or visit our website at
www.ionabooks.com
for details of all our products and online sales